Struggle for

(Note this conversation was recorded on Oct 22, 2023 in Salt Lake City, Utah. The interview has been lightly edited for clarity.)

Introduction

Dr Sara Patterson is the author of "The Sept 6 & the Struggle for the Soul of Mormonism." She thinks we should think about more people than just the 6 excommunicated in September of 1993. We'll discuss Janice Allred, Sonia Johnson, David Wright, and even Mark Hofmann! Check out our conversation...

Tags: Gospel Tangents, Rick Bennett, LDS Church, Latter-day Saints, LDS Church, Mormon, Mormon Church, Church of Jesus Christ of Latter-day Saints, Mormon history, Mormon, LDS Church, LDS, Church of Latter Day Saints, Michael Quinn, Paul Toscano, Margaret Toscano, Sara Patterson, David Wright, Brent Metcalfe, Avraham Gileadi, purity culture, intellectualism, academic freedom, BYU, David Knowlton, excommunicated, BYU Studies, September 6, Mormonism, martyr, family, feminism, Sonia, ERA, Mark Hofmann, feminists, women, hierarchy, ultra conservative, excommunicated, campus, Cecilia Konchar Farr, equal rights amendment, professor, scholarship, tenure, Gail Houston

Contents

Michael Quinn: Tragedy or Triumph?

Interview

GT 00:41 Welcome to *Gospel Tangents*. I'm excited to have an amazing, at least new to me, historian, could you go ahead and tell us who you are and where you teach?

Sara 00:50 Sure. I'm Sara Patterson. And I teach at Hanover College in Southern Indiana.

GT 00:55 Southern Indiana. Are you a Hoosier?

Sara 00:58 I guess so. {both laughing}

GT 01:02 Well, one of the things I always like to do is, I like to get people's backgrounds. Where did you get your Bachelor's and master's and Ph.D. and all that stuff?

Sara 01:10 I received my undergraduate degree from Denison University in Ohio. And then I went to Claremont Graduate School for my doctorate.

GT 01:20 Oh, was that with Patrick Mason?[1]

Sara 01:23 I was there before Patrick.

GT 01:25 Oh, so Dr. Bushman?[2]

Sara 01:27 No, I studied with Ann Taves. And on my dissertation committee, Jan Shipps was a member.

GT 01:34 Oh, wow. That's cool.

---

[1] See https://gospeltangents.com/people/patrick-mason/
[2] See https://gospeltangents.com/people/richard-bushman/

Sara 01:36 Yeah.

GT 01:36 I just thought it was Bushman and then Patrick Mason, I didn't know Ann Taves was in there.

Sara 01:41 I was there when they were fundraising for that chair.

GT 01:43 Okay. Was Ann before Richard Bushman, then?

Sara 01:52 I want to say she overlapped with him one year, and then she went to UC Santa Barbara.

GT 01:57 Oh, wow. I did not know that. Wow. So, you're an old timer then in Mormon studies, right?

Sara 02:02 Yeah, I guess so.

GT 02:03 Except for, did you major in Mormon studies, or was it just religious studies? Tell us more about your studies.

Sara 02:11 My degree is in history, but I specialized in religious history in the United States. And so, Mormonism has always been an interest of mine.

GT 02:19 Okay, because you're not Mormon.

Sara 02:22 I'm not.

GT 02:23 And so how did you get interested in Mormon studies?

Sara 02:26 It was just through the study of religion in the United States. And in reading about the early church, I was just captivated by the story.

GT 02:37 Okay.

Sara 02:38 Yeah.

GT 02:38 I talked to Cristina Rosetti.[3] Do you know, Cristina?

Sara 02:41 Yeah.

GT 02:41 She said that, kind of like Parley P. Pratt, she opened up *Rough Stone Rolling*,[4] and she read it all night. {both chuckling} Did you have any experiences like that?

Sara 02:50 I don't think I would characterize it that way. That's great. {both laughing} It was more of a slow growing interest in me.

GT 02:59 Okay. When you were six years old, you probably didn't say I'm going to grow up as a religious studies scholar?

Sara 03:08 I did not.

GT 03:08 How did that development happen?

Sara 03:14 In college, I took a required religion class. And it just opened my eyes. I've always been interested, I think, in why people do and act, the ways that they do. And so, the religion class just helped me see religion as a motivator for people. And I was just hooked at that point.

GT 03:39 Okay.

Sara 03:39 Yeah.

GT 03:40 And so, do you have any other interests besides Mormonism?

---

[3] See https://gospeltangents.com/people/cristina-rosetti/
[4] Can be purchased at https://amzn.to/3jevhQ3

Sara 03:46 Yeah, I'm interested more broadly in gender and sexuality in religion, and then also in material culture and sacred spaces. One of my first major projects was about a piece of outsider art in Southern California. I did a project it's out in the middle of the desert. So, I interviewed people who are coming to visit that space called Salvation Mountain. And I was just interested in how the artists and the people who visited created sacred space together.

GT 04:23 Okay. Well, very good. And so, then you got your first job in Indiana, and that's why you're there now. Is that right?

Sara 04:30 Yeah, it was my first tenure track job.

GT 04:33 Okay.

Sara 04:33 Yeah.

GT 04:34 All right.

Sara 04:35 So that's why I'm there now.

GT 04:36 All right. Well, it's interesting. You've written a new book, why don't you go ahead and show everybody the book and tell us how you got involved in this book?

Sara 04:48 Am I holding it up correctly?

GT 04:49 You're doing a very good job.

Sara 04:50 Okay, I'll tell you how I got involved. For those who aren't watching, what's it called?

Sara 04:55 The September Six and the Struggle for the Soul of Mormonism.[5]

GT 04:58 Okay.

Sara 05:03 I would say a couple of things. Perhaps most recently, I was asked to be part of a conference, maybe two years ago now that Ben Park helped put together that was honoring the life and contributions of Mike Quinn.[6]

GT 05:21 Oh, that was here at University of Utah. Right?

Sara 05:24 Yes, it was.

GT 05:25 I was at that conference.

Sara 05:26 Okay. Well, I gave a paper there. {both chuckling} And studying more about Quinn, who is somebody that I met in graduate school, because he was a friend of one of my professors. That just really drew me into this time period in new ways. And so when Barbara Jones Brown[7] at Signature [Books] talked to me about doing a book more broadly about the September Six, I was really excited for that opportunity.

GT 05:58 Okay. Michael Quinn drew you in, and then you've expanded it to the others.

Sara 06:02 That's right. I'd known about the September Six for a long time, but, yeah, reading more about Quinn's life just really drew me in.

GT 06:12 Well, it must be interesting. Mormons are often very insular. And so, when you first heard about the September Six, I

---

[5] Can be purchased at https://amzn.to/3t1Aodc
[6] See https://gospeltangents.com/people/michael-quinn/
[7] See https://gospeltangents.com/people/barbara-jones-brown/

8

mean, I don't know, if you have a religious background, like if, you're Orthodox, Baptist or whatever. Does it look really strange that this church out here in Utah is excommunicating a bunch of intellectuals? How did you come across that story? What were your reactions?

Sara 06:41 I think that I had been studying the history of Christianity for long enough that it wasn't shocking to me that a church would do that. I mean, I think that religious institutions, that's one of the ways that they can manage the boundaries in their communities. And so, I think it was intriguing to me that it's something that was happening so recently, because you tend to think of excommunications as a method of the past, though they certainly do.

GT 07:11 Galileo. {both laughing}

Sara 07:11 I wasn't even thinking that far back. But yeah, so I think that excommunications, that story draws people in, I think, because it's such a severe measure.

GT 07:30 Yeah, I would agree with that.

Sara 07:31 Yeah.

GT 07:32 I have a Jewish friend, and he told me you cannot be excommunicated from Judaism, even for murder. Because under their rule, or logic, I guess, God is to be your judge. And so, Christianity hasn't followed that same tact. I mean the Catholic Church. But you familiar with other churches that excommunicate people for not following the pure doctrine or whatever?

Sara 08:05 I think most of the examples I know of are within Christianity.

GT 08:08 Okay.

Sara 08:08 Yeah.

GT 08:09 But, I mean, the Catholic Church, I guess, is big. And I guess that we've got the Salem witch trials, maybe.

Sara 08:15 Yeah.

GT 08:15 Are there other examples besides those even more recent?

Sara 08:18 Oh sure. There's a Catholic theologian, whose name I will probably butcher because I've only ever read it. I haven't heard it. But his last name is Soraya M Bella. And he wrote a book about Mary that's really fascinating, and [he] was disciplined and I think excommunicated for it.

GT 08:42 Okay.

Sara 08:43 Yeah.

GT 08:44 But that's another Catholic example. Right?

Sara 08:46 Yeah, relatively recently. {both chuckling}

GT 08:50 All right. Yeah, I just wish excommunication would go away, personally, but it doesn't seem like it has, at least in the LDS church. Can you talk a little bit more about how Michael Quinn drew you in and then how it expanded into the September Six?

Sara 09:11 Sure, I was able to read portions of his journal and memoir when I was working on my presentation for the Quinn conference. That ultimately wasn't what I focused on in my presentation. What I focused on was how we today narrate Quinn's life, and what I think is a problematic way of telling his life story, that talks about him as a rising star. Then after his excommunication, frames his life as a series of losses. I was pushing back against that narrative because I think it uses the Church's lens to read his life story.

GT 10:01 Okay.

Sara 10:03 And so part of what I was looking at was how Quinn reconstructed his family and restructured his family, how he created community in places like Affirmation.[8] And how, while we may think that his life didn't live up to understandings of family that might be ideal, and he didn't ever find a long-term partner, that his life wasn't a series of losses I was saying. We don't need to read him as a tragic figure. We can certainly see that there were hardships and tragedies in his life, but also acknowledge that he continued to live a rich life after his excommunication.

GT 10:55 You know, I'm glad you went there. Because that's something that I think those of us who are still in the LDS Church, look at. Here he is. He's one of the most popular teachers at BYU. Everything's going really well. He's had some experiences with President Kimball. And then he gets excommunicated. And then he loses his job at BYU. He's never able to get another tenure track position, anywhere. It seems like he's forced out of some positions. I think he taught at Yale for a year or two. I think [he taught at] Arizona State maybe as well. But it does look from an inside perspective, that he has had a series of losses, it was pretty devastating to him. And so, it's interesting to hear from you to say we need to look at this from another way. I know that in some respects, among the more critical crowd, he's seen as a hero. A lot of his writings have kind of triumphed in a way. And so, he's kind of, I hate to use the word ex-Mormon hero in a way, but he's still a believer, up through his death, a very, very strong believer. So, tell us more about why you're pushing back against that narrative that I just gave.

---

[8] See https://affirmation.org/

Sara 12:24 Well, I think, as I said briefly, that it uses the Church's measuring stick of what a life is supposed to be. And so, I think that we need to expand our understanding of what rich life can be, beyond that set of expectations. Because he continued to have faith. He talked about having a fulfilling life. He talked about himself as a mystic, and as a member of a church of one. But he talked about how he continued to have a very close relationship with God and continued to feel connected to the Spirit. I think that we have to include that in the story, even when his relationship with the institution was so painful, because it's a mixed bag. Right? And, I think too often, sometimes to try to get him into the category of martyr.

GT 13:41 Right.

Sara 13:44 The last part of his life.

GT 13:45 He does seem like a martyr.

Sara 13:46 Yeah, I think a lot of people do see him as a martyr. But I think too often to get him into that narrative, people talk about his life as a series of losses, and things that he lost because he was willing to stand up and speak the truth. But one of the things I talked about was, once he left the church, he was able to ask research questions that he wanted to ask. Right? There's a freedom that he had in his intellectual life that opened up. And so, I just think that there's complexity that gets lost sometimes in forcing him into that martyr story.

GT 14:31 Okay. Could we call his life a life of abundance? And if so, what would be some of those abundant things? I mean, you did mention he could study more freely. Are there other things besides that?

Sara 14:44 I think his spiritual life, I think people tend to focus on the disintegration of his family. When years after he came out to his wife, and [people] don't talk about the fact that they restructured their family and so he spent his holidays with his ex-wife and his children. So, I think a broader understanding of family is necessary, for thinking about his relationships.

GT 15:20 So even though his marriage went away, he was still able to embrace his ex-wife and family and have a good life with them.

Sara 15:27 Yeah.

GT 15:28 Which is pretty unusual.

Sara 15:30 Yeah, she wanted him to be part of his children's lives. And he was.

GT 15:37 Very good.

Untold Story of David Wright

Interview

GT 00:35 One of the other things that I thought was very interesting about your book, you felt like it should be more than just six and maybe we should mention who the six are. And then who are the other people that you think should be added into those six or eight or 10 or 12?

Sara 00:51 Yeah, sure. {both chuckling} The six are Lynne Whitesides,[9] Avraham Gileadi, Paul Toscano,[10] Maxine Hanks, Lavina Fielding Anderson, and Mike Quinn.[11]

GT 01:06 Oh, very good. I always stumble over those. So very good.

Sara 01:12 I think that part of what I'm trying to argue in the book is that the idea of the September Six locks us into a particular narrative, and that we need to look more expansively beyond that month to see a decade's long process within the church, to try to pull people towards an orthodoxy and a unity. So, there are certainly others that I focus on in the book. David Wright is one of them. He was excommunicated, about six months after the September Six. He wondered if he was originally supposed to be part of that group. And then because of kind of individual circumstances, it was delayed.

GT 02:08 He's a former BYU professor as well, right?

Sara 02:10 That's right.

---

[9] See https://gospeltangents.com/people/lynne-whitesides/
[10] See https://gospeltangents.com/people/paul-toscano/
[11] See https://gospeltangents.com/people/michael-quinn/

GT 02:11 His story isn't very well known, I don't think.

Sara 02:15 No, it isn't. When I interviewed him, one of the things he said is, I usually only merit one sentence in discussions about the September Six. And so, would you like me to talk a little bit?

GT 02:30 Well, he was your introduction, basically.

Sara 02:32 He was my introduction, in part because I wanted to start the book, outside of the month, just to begin by disrupting the stories that people normally tell about that month. He was a Biblical Studies professor. And he initially in his career wanted to be the next Hugh Nibley. So, he set out to be a defender of the faith and an apologist for the church. Over the course of his studies, he talked about, for a long time pushing, trying to avoid this, but came to believe that Mormon scriptures weren't historical documents or weren't ancient texts. And so, what he was trying to do was embrace the method of historical criticism. And also see in the text, a broader meaning. He was trying to create a faithful approach to the Scriptures that didn't rely on the historicity of the texts. He got a lot of pushback for that and was eventually excommunicated.

Sara 04:06 One of the stories that really struck me in his own experiences, he could tell that his interactions with his bishop and stake president weren't going anywhere. But he really wanted to participate in the baptism of one of his sons and the ordination into the Aaronic priesthood of another son. And so, he was trying to delay what he felt was the inevitable. They eventually decided that he couldn't participate in those sacraments. He had to stand off to the side. He talked about how hard that was for him, especially as part of a family that had generations of Mormons in it to be sidelined from these really important events in his sons' lives. And so, I started the book with him to try to upset the September Six framing right from the beginning. And I think that some of the people at BYU who were disciplined during that same time period, are important to think about. Ultimately, I would say, I wouldn't choose another number.

GT 05:35 I wanted to get a number out of you. {both laughing}

Sara 05:38 Yeah, I appreciate that. But I think that we need to look at the disciplining of a number of people more broadly and disciplining in different ways; so not all excommunications, but some people losing their positions at BYU, some people just being called in over and over again for their scholarship by their local bishops and stake presidents.

GT 06:10 Yeah. Can you talk about some of those people? David Knowlton, I think, is one of them.

Sara 06:14 Sure, David Knowlton was a professor at BYU, along with Cecilia Konchar Farr, and Gail Houston, all three of them in 1992, were up for review for their teaching positions, and the question was whether they would have continuing status.

GT 06:41 Which is like tenure in a way?

Sara 06:44 The closest to tenure that you can get at BYU.

GT 06:47 Right.

Sara 06:47 Yeah. And all three of them were denied continuing status, and so had one more year in their positions, and then asked to leave.

GT 07:00 And maybe for those who aren't in academia, like you and I...

Sara 07:03 Yeah.

GT 07:04 They might not understand why tenure is a good thing, or at least from an academic point of view. Let's talk a little bit about tenure and how that's a little bit different at BYU.

16

Sara 07:16 Sure. Tenure exists to help protect the academic freedom of intellectuals, so that institutions can't punish them for the questions that they're asking, or the research that they're doing. And so, that doesn't exist at BYU, I think, because it's a religious institution. And so, the idea of academic freedom has always been more complicated at BYU, because it's a religious institution. And so, I think it's clear that at various times at BYU, there have been limitations on the questions that people could ask or the research that they would be able to do. So, the focus in Knowlton's case was tied to his research. And for Farr, it really revolved around her participation in a pro-choice rally in Salt Lake City, where she stood up and said, "I'm a Mormon and I'm pro-choice." I think really interestingly, she had been asked by a student in one of her classes to participate in this rally. She understood that that could be a controversial thing. She also understood why it could also be a powerful thing to have a BYU professor say that she was pro-choice. So, she went to her bishop and stake president and told them, "Here's what I am planning on doing. This is this speech that I'm going to give. You know me and you know that I'm a faithful person". And they both said, "Okay." So, she went off and participated in the rally. And then the backlash that she received was at BYU. She never was excommunicated.

GT 09:43 Okay.

Sara 09:43 Because, at least the way that she talks about it, is that the bishop and the Stake President defended her and refused to do anything. Because they had had this exchange about what she was going to do and because they knew that she was a faithful person, and that she saw this as an important stance to take. So, in my interview with her, she talked about how it was two men who stood between her and excommunication, which is, I think, a really powerful statement that she was just, even 30 years later, she remembered that as a really meaningful thing. They didn't attempt to discipline her.

17

GT 10:36 Did she have any indication that the higher ups wanted to have her excommunicated?

Sara 10:43 Well, I think what happened at BYU, at least indicated to her that what she had done was seen as a problem.

GT 10:50 Okay.

Sara 10:51 She was called in after the rally by her department chair. She remembers that part of what they were talking about was whether or not BYU should or could say what a faculty member should talk about when they're off campus. Yeah. And the department chair said that she should not speak again about the issues. Then, there was a feminist newspaper in Salt Lake City that asked to republish her speech, and she agreed to that. The department chair took that as her choosing to speak again, basically...

GT 11:47 Oh, okay.

Sara 11:48 ...on the topic. It was complicated, because then there's the academic review process. Some of what was happening was framed that her scholarship wasn't up to the standards of the school.

GT 12:10 Meaning it was too political? Or, I mean, is it one of those things where they're like, "well, your scholarships not really good," but it was fine. It really was a cover for politics.

Sara 12:24 Yes. The latter. She ended up suing BYU. There was a legal settlement.

GT 12:37 So, it sounds like she won the legal settlement even if she lost her job.

Sara 12:40 That's right. These cases are all really complicated. But the issue of academic freedom is a really complicated issue on BYU's campus.

GT 12:59 So is this a case with David Knowlton? Cecilia Farr? Isn't there a Robert Rees as well? I'm trying to remember. You said another name.

Sara 13:09 Ah, Gail Houston.

GT 13:11 Gail Houston. Is this a case where "well, we won't go after your membership? We'll just go after your paycheck." Whereas they didn't really because we haven't talked about Margaret[12] and Paul Toscano[13] yet. Margaret, I joked with her, "Are you six and a half or seven?"

Sara 13:28 Yeah. {both laughing}

GT 13:30 Because she was really in the thick of that, too. But she wasn't a BYU employee. I don't believe.

GT 13:35 No she was not. Oh, wait.

GT 13:36 Oh she did teach adjunct I guess.

Sara 13:38 That's right. She was not. I'd have to check.

GT 13:42 But I know by the year.

Sara 13:43 Yeah.

GT 13:43 We're jumping ahead on the story a little bit because she didn't get excommunicated till 2000. She got in trouble in '93 with

---

[12] See https://gospeltangents.com/people/Margaret-toscano/
[13] See https://gospeltangents.com/people/paul-toscano/

the rest. But because she continued to publish, they couldn't do anything about her job. Is that why they went after her membership? Could we look at it that way?

Sara 14:00 Oh, that's interesting. I think part of the reason that the BYU professors were disciplined is that BYU has been imagined as a place of believers building Zion as like an example for the rest of the world. And so, there's been an impulse, I think, from the administration to want it to be the best example of orthodoxy and to want it to have the campus present a unified message about what being a faithful person looks like. And so, I think that was the danger with these faculty people because they were suggesting that they could be faithful and have other ideas and do other things than what was expected of them.

GT 15:09 I mean, it's interesting because Michael Quinn worked at BYU. Was fired from BYU and got excommunicated. So, he got everything.

Sara 15:15 He wasn't fired from BYU. He resigned.

GT 15:17 Well, he resigned, but resigned under pressure.

Sara 15:21 He definitely saw the writing on the wall. Yeah.

GT 15:23 Yeah. Because he had reached, I don't know the status at BYU, but the equivalent of tenured status at BYU.

Sara 15:33 Right.

GT 15:34 And so, but that didn't protect him when he wrote about women holding the priesthood in 1843.[14] I know that was one of the articles that was cited in his excommunication.

---

[14] See https://gospeltangents.com/2018/08/women-have-priesthood-since-1843/

Sara 15:45 That came out after he left.

GT 15:48 Oh, was that after?

Sara 15:48 Yeah, he left BYU in '88. And that came out in '93.

The Untold Story of David Wright

Interview

GT 15:53 Okay, so it's interesting. I always wonder, Lynne Whitesides[15] is another one. She was disfellowshipped, never excommunicated.

Sara 16:02 Yeah.

GT 16:03 And I even asked her I'm like, they went after Margaret, seven years later. Why are you still a member? I mean, she doesn't go to church.

Sara 16:12 Right.

GT 16:12 She's not, I wouldn't even call her believer at all.

Sara 16:15 Right.

GT 16:15 Whereas, Margaret still is.

Sara 16:17 Well, I think Lynne's a different type of believer. You know, she's moved away from the church totally.

GT 16:21 Yeah, well she's moved away from Christianity.

Sara 16:23 Yeah. And I think she fairly quickly came to view her dis-fellowship-ment as freedom or liberation.

GT 16:34 Yeah, she definitely did.

---

[15] See https://gospeltangents.com/people/lynne-whitesides

Sara 16:36 From and felt like she found a much more fulfilling spiritual life outside of the institution.

GT 16:44 So it was just interesting. Quinn lost or resigned from his job, but under pressure. So I'm going to say, to me, I treat that as a loss.

Sara 16:54 Okay. {both chuckling}

GT 16:56 Then he was excommunicated. They went after Margaret. They went after Janice Allred,[16] who we haven't talked about yet.

Sara 17:02 Yeah.

GT 17:02 I think you've included her in the September group. You have a broader picture. But it's interesting how Cecilia Farr, David Knowlton, are still members. Was just going after their job good enough? Or why haven't they been excommunicated as well? I guess that is my question? Why did they go after David Wright and Michael Quinn and not some of these others? Do you have any insight into that?

Sara 17:33 I would be hypothesizing, of course.

GT 17:36 We can do that. This is *Gospel Tangents*. I know that historians don't like to do that. But I do! I like it when we do that!

Sara 17:47 It makes me anxious. {both laughing} Could it have happened differently? I always think, I don't know.

GT 17:56 It's called Monday morning quarterback.

---

16 See https://gospeltangents.com/people/janice-allred/

Sara 17:57 Cecilia left Utah, and found another position. She left with her temple recommend in her hand. She stayed in the church for quite some time. In fact, it wasn't until her children were struggling with some of the messages in the church that she decided to stop attending church.

GT 18:22 Okay.

Sara 18:25 But, perhaps it has to do with her moving away from those centers of orthodoxy. She moved to the Midwest. She talked about feeling initially, when people still remembered who she was, in terms of the BYU story, that women would ask her questions. She felt like they were trying to feel out. Where's the line so that I make sure that I don't cross it? But I think moving away helps. Right?

GT 19:01 It didn't help Kate Kelly, but that's beyond... {Rick laughing}

Sara 19:06 See, this is why I don't do hypothetical stuff {both laughing}. I'm forgetting who else you included in your question.

GT 19:18 One person that I'm not as familiar with, that you had mentioned was Gail Houston. Let's learn more about her story.

Sara 19:26 I don't know a whole lot about it. It wasn't a story that I focused on in the book. But she also was involved with feminist issues on campus, and I believe that that was what the issue was.

GT 19:39 Okay. And she was pretty good friends with Cecilia?

Sara 19:43 They both worked with VOICE, which was a feminist student group. And VOICE was quite active on BYU's campus and was receiving a lot of pushback. And so, I think that what they were doing was seen as a lightning rod, activist group on campus.

GT 20:06 And we don't do activism in the church.

24

Sara 20:09 Well, yeah. One of the issues that they were talking about at that time was assault on BYU's campus.

GT 20:22 Sexual assault.

Sara 20:23 [Yes.] It's clear from letters to the editor, they had a flyer that was meant to be ironic. There was a woman who was attacked on campus one morning at, I don't know, 10 in the morning. I think she was beat up a little bit but managed to get away from the attacker. In response, they made a flyer that said, "Starting immediately, there's going to be a curfew for men on BYU's campus." I don't know. It was 10pm or something. And after that time, men need to walk with at least two women, if they're going to be out to show that they're not a threat to anybody. People really responded negatively to that. I think that they failed to see what they were trying to communicate, which was that women often don't feel safe on campus and feel like they need to travel in groups. But in letters to the editor about that, it's very clear. This goes back to this idea that BYU is a special place. And so, it's very clear that any kind of assault that was happening on the campus was outsiders coming onto the campus.

GT 22:05 Not insiders.

Sara 22:06 Assaulting people, yes. So, people were just very reluctant to even entertain the idea that assault might happen. Student on student assault might happen. And so yeah, I think that's tied to how people want to imagine BYU.

GT 22:25 Well, and I know BYU, it seems like if I remember right, when Elder Holland was president of BYU, he wanted to make it Harvard of the West. But there's some problems with that. Harvard allows Jewish scholars, Catholic scholars, Protestant scholars. BYU doesn't. You have to be LDS. Well, I won't say you have to be, but they don't have a Jewish scholar teaching Judaism. They don't have a Methodist scholar teaching Methodism. That's against the rules. Doesn't it seem like there's a conflict with being the Harvard of the West when we are not really acting like Harvard or Notre Dame, or some of these other schools that allow non-Catholic faculty, for example, at Notre Dame to teach Judaism or Islam or Methodism or whatever? Can you talk about that tension at BYU?

Sara 23:29 Well, I think David Wright is an interesting example of that, because it was because of Holland's statement about the Harvard of the West that he decided to go to BYU. He had several job offers. And he thought, if I can go to BYU and do this scholarship, that is, historical criticism was just part of scriptural studies. He was not at all radical or cutting edge in terms of what he was saying about Scripture and how it should be read.

GT 24:06 But he was radical at BYU.

Sara 24:08 But, he was radical at BYU. And so, when he got there, he quickly realized that he was not able to have the conversations that he wanted to have. He talked about wanting to host a discussion of differences between creation stories, and the response he got from his department members was, "don't point out to people that there are differences in the creation stories because, if they don't know that, then you don't want to introduce to them something that might become a problem for their faith." And so, yes, I think it's not just tied to different faiths teaching their own perspectives, but it's also about what questions you're able to ask. And I think he didn't realize that people were going to perceive at a basic level in introductory Biblical Studies classes you learn that there are differences in the creation stories at secular universities all around the country. So, yeah, it was radical, as you said.

Sonia Johnson & ERA

Interview

GT 00:35 Let's talk a little bit about some of the other people. I was surprised in your book that you even went back to Sonia Johnson. For those who aren't familiar with Sonia Johnson, because they're not as old as say I am, give the young people an idea of who was Sonia Johnson and why was she a problem for the church?

Sara 00:57 Sonia Johnson was a church member who fought for the Equal Rights Amendment. And she talked about the Equal Rights Amendment when she first heard that phrase, Equal Rights Amendment, she said something like "the three most beautiful words in the English language." So, she really felt like the ERA was an important issue, and that it didn't contradict her faith. She was an activist for the ERA. She was one of the founders of Mormons for the ERA. And she was eventually excommunicated for that work. Part of the reason that I talk about her is because the Equal Rights Amendment was one of the, I think, defining moments for the church hierarchy in terms of how it would talk about political issues. So, what the church hierarchy said about the Equal Rights Amendment was more generally, excuse me. I should start there, more generally, it said, "we're not going to get into political issues." But it framed the Equal Rights Amendment as a moral issue. And therefore said, "we can absolutely say that this is a problem for society." So, the Church very actively worked against the Equal Rights Amendment, once it had been framed as a moral issue.

Sara 2:44 Part of what happened with Sonia Johnson, is that church leaders started to frame feminism as an external foreign movement that was trying to infiltrate the church and Church leaders narrated it as, "this is going to upset the family." And because we, as the Church, care about the family, we need to protect the family. And the family needs to be a heterosexual union with the man being the provider and protector and priesthood holder, and the woman

27

being the nurturer, and caretaker of the home and wife. So, what the fear that they were saying was that the Equal Rights Amendment would upset that family structure because it would collapse the differences between men and women. Then they talked about it as having this snowballing effect. So, if the differences between men and women collapsed, then divorce rates were going to go up. Children weren't going to be raised in a moral household. There would be more teen pregnancy and abortion. Men would feel like they weren't men anymore, so they might have affairs. Those affairs might with be with other men, so it was this snowball effect, because they were arguing the family was the foundation. Right?

Sara 4:35 And so basically, the moral structure of society would crumble if the Equal Rights Amendment passed. I think it was during that Equal Rights Amendment era that Church leaders got this theology framed that would then suit them well as they continued on into the 80s and 90s, talking about feminism as a danger to the Church. Once they were able to make the claim that feminism was outside the Church trying to get in, then they could also make the claim that they had to be the boundary enforcers to try to protect the family.

GT 05:29 And so by excommunicating Sonia, they made her an outsider, an outside threat?

Sara 05:36 Right.

GT 05:36 Instead of an inside threat.

Sara 05:38 Yeah. And that excommunication really cast a chill over Mormon feminism, which was really interesting. Women were asking really interesting questions about what their roles were, about the theology of the church, and Sonia Johnson served as this lesson.

GT 06:08 Was she the canary in the coal mine?

Sara 06:12 There are certain things you shouldn't be doing and talking about, yes.

GT 06:15 Because, was she excommunicated in 1982? Does that sound right to you?

Sara 06:20 I want to say it was 1979.

GT 06:21 Was it '79? So, it was even earlier.

Sara 06:23 Yeah.

GT 06:24 Because, I remember looking at that and saying, "Well, 79 to 93. That's 14 years. That's a big gap". But could we say that, I mean, even though Sonia, she's more focused on ERA, and you look at somebody like Maxine Hanks, Margaret Toscano, more of feminist theology. Can we see Sonia as influencing them. And that's why they had to go after Maxine and Margaret and Janice and people like that?

Sara 06:59 I talk about Sonia actually in a chapter about the Church hierarchy. I think part of what I think was happening with Sonia Johnson and the Equal Rights Amendment, is the Church hierarchy was telling and reinforcing these narratives about feminism, and about the family and developing strategies for working on political issues. So, when the issue of same sex marriage came up later, the same thing happened in terms of we're going to frame this as a moral issue that's threatening the family. And so therefore, we can speak about what is a political issue but framing it in a moral way. I think all of that was forged in that Equal Rights Amendment era, how the church was going to approach feminism, but also these issues that it wanted to frame as moral.

GT 08:07 Well, it's interesting you say that. I know there was a, I'm trying to decide if I should say the person's name. I'll just say a BYU professor for now.

Sara 08:16 Okay.

GT 08:17 I'll keep it generic. [This professor] talked a lot about Sonia Johnson, and also the gay rights movement, and that the church was always trying to say, "Well, if we allow feminism to influence the culture, gay rights is the next domino." And as we look at Elder Packers 19...

Sara 08:39 It was 1993.

GT 08:42 Was it 93? So it was the same year.

Sara 08:44 It was May 1993.

GT 08:45 Because he said that the biggest problems were feminists, intellectuals and gays.

Sara 08:52 Yeah.

GT 08:52 He didn't say it in those words.

Sara 08:53 He said the gay lesbian movement.

GT 08:55 Yeah. And so, the gay lesbian movement has always been tied to feminism as to create a boogeyman. I mean, I don't see Margaret, Janice, who was the other one I just mentioned? [Maxine.] To me, they were more feminist theologians. They weren't looking at the politics, but the church always seemed to collapse them. Is that why they were seen as threats, even though they weren't pushing necessarily for ERA?

Sara 09:27 Well, yes. I think that because they were feminists, I mean, I think they share similarities. So, I'll talk about them together, but they had different projects that they were working on. I think Heavenly Mother was an issue that the Church hierarchy clearly didn't want people exploring. And so, when Janice Allred was exploring heavenly mother or when Margaret Toscano gave a presentation at BYU about the feminine divine, the Church hierarchy had already said this wasn't something that they wanted people talking about. They were women who were saying, "I can talk about it. And I can think creatively about how this theology might work." And so, they were claiming a spiritual authority that I think was threatening to the Church hierarchy.

GT 10:31 Especially, since they didn't hold the priesthood because they were women, for heaven's sake. Right?

Sara 10:35 Right. Margaret was also talking about women in the priesthood. And so, I think that they were challenging. They were feminists who are challenging what the Church hierarchy had already drawn boundaries around.

GT 10:54 So just feminism is bad, whether it's in the political arena of ERA or theological arena of Heavenly Mother or women in priesthood.

Sara 11:03 Yeah.

GT 11:04 This is just [bad.] We can't have it.

Sara 11:05 And part of what I think happened, which I talk about in my chapter about the Toscano's is, I think that Margaret and Paul had a marriage that was structured differently than the Church expected marriages to be structured. Here was Margaret, who was speaking with authority about spiritual matters. And here was Paul, who, when they met with their stake president, he was unwilling to rein in his wife in fact...

31

GT 11:42 "Can't you get her under control?"

Sara 11:43 He went after the local leaders, instead of reining her in.

GT 11:47 Reining in his wife.

Sara 11:48 Which I think was their expectation. Right? We'll have them both here. And then, they'll stop.

GT 11:56 Paul would put his thumb on her head.

Sara 11:57 Right. I think that while they were both making much broader arguments that were problematic for the church. They also were just not living up to gender expectations. I think that was really frustrating to the local hierarchy.

Brent Metcalfe & Mark Hofmann

Interview

GT 12:20 Are there any other people? We've talked about the six. We've added David Wright, Cecilia Farr, Gail Houston, Margaret technically wasn't part of the six.

Sara 12:36 Right.

GT 12:36 Her sister, Janice Allred. So that's, we're up to like, 10 now. Right?

Sara 12:42 Right. You're trying to get me to say a number. {chuckling}

GT 12:45 See, I'm a numbers guy. I'm a math guy.

Sara 12:47 Did we add Brent Metcalfe in there?

GT 12:48 Oh, Brent Metcalfe. That was another one. I was going to mention him.

Sara 12:51 Yeah.

GT 12:52 Let's talk a little bit about Brent.

Sara 12:54 Well, he...

GT 12:55 By the way Brent, you need to come on my podcast! {both chuckling}

Sara 12:59 He had a collection of essays that came out, I think, in 94, called <u>New Approaches to the Book of Mormon</u>.[17] It contained an essay by David Wright. It was a group of people studying scripture, many of whom were arguing that the Book of Mormon was not an ancient text. So, it was the same set of issues that I talked about with David.

GT 13:24 But it still provides value. It's not like they were trying to knock it down as worthless.

Sara 13:29 Right.

GT 13:30 Or just fiction.

Sara 13:31 Right. And that was something that in biblical studies, those arguments had been made for a long time that...

GT 13:42 Regarding the Bible.

Sara 13:44 Regarding biblical texts, absolutely, that you can read the text. You can read that text as history, but scholars were arguing that it doesn't hold up to historical criticism. But there were a lot of scholars who are saying, there can be lots of metaphors and meaning that can still be taken from the text. And this text can still be seen as inspired, while also accounting for human hands in the text. So, in terms of scriptural studies, they weren't making cases that were new, but they were trying to help create a faithful approach to the Book of Mormon.

GT 14:32 Well, and Brent is especially interesting because he was in the crosshairs because he was, he knew Mark Hofmann[18] quite well.

Sara 14:41 Right.

---

[17] Can be purchased at https://amzn.to/48eXDQZ
[18] See https://gospeltangents.com/lds_people_historical/mark-hofmann/

GT 14:42 And so there was that whole issue where he was viewed as a suspect potentially in some of those murders.[19] Clearly, he had nothing to do with them now. But at the time, and then in the 1980s that was a question. Then you said it was '94 when he published this new book. Was that the straw that broke the camel's back? Do you talk much about the Hofmann stuff with Brent Metcalfe?

Sara 15:09 No, I talk about Brent Metcalfe more with David Wright, than in my section about Mark Hofmann. {both chuckling} But part of why I talk about Hofmann in the book is because I think that the events around him made Church leaders aware of and anxious about history telling. Not that they hadn't already been, but I think what happened with Hofmann raised those questions in a new way.

GT 15:44 So can we conclude Mark Hofmann as part of the September Six as well?

Sara 15:48 No. (emphatically) No, we cannot. {both laughing}

GT 15:53 He's a whole other story. When you get murder, that kicks you out of the group? {Rick laughing}

---

[19] See https://gospeltangents.com/mormon_history/hofmann-bombingsforgeries/

Ultra-Conservatives Exed?

Interview

GT 16:00 Who were some of the other people that you would put in the broader September Six category?

Sara 16:09 Those are the names that initially spring to mind. Another issue that I talk about is the excommunications around the same time of ultra-conservative church members.

GT 16:20 Okay.

Sara 16:23 Part of what I'm thinking about in that discussion is Avraham Gileadi. Because he's the member of the September Six, that doesn't fit what I would see as more general patterns. I think that his inclusion in the September Six was about the fact that his excommunication happened that month. People wanted to communicate that this was a big deal. This was a really intense set of actions on the Church leaders. Part that Gileadi, from the Church leaders perspective was more connected to these ultra conservative members, and his work was being used by them to support the arguments that they were making.

GT 17:18 Are there others like Bo Gritz that we could include in there?

Sara 17:22 Yes. Not in the September Six.

GT 17:25 Well, I mean, in the broader movement.

Sara 17:27 Yes. Yes. Bo Gritz, Jim and Elaine Harmston, Sterling Allen.

GT 17:34 Okay.

Sara 17:35 Yeah.

How Intellectuals Have Moved the Church

Interview

GT 00:31 So you, with your book, you're way more expansive than just those six individuals who got "exed."

Sara 00:39 I am, yeah.

GT 00:40 And I noticed the subtitle is *The Struggle for the Soul of Mormonism.*

Sara 00:45 [Yes.]

GT 00:46 Can you talk about, has anything happened with regards to the September Six, that has changed the leadership as far as moving more towards them?

Sara 01:03 Can you say the end part of that question again? Moving the church leaders more towards?

GT 01:11 Yeah, so for example, I know with Mark Hofmann, and I know we don't want to include him in there. But it does seem to many, I would say, that there's been a more openness to discussions of polygamy, and magic and seer stones. And so, it does seem like, even though Mark Hofmann was a terrible person, there has been first a closing and then an opening into church history. Do you see any of the same sort of things with feminism or these other issues, historicity of the Book of Mormon. Has it changed church leaders?

Sara 01:51 I see. So, have the ideas that were presented by the six become more mainstream?

GT 01:59 Mainstream.

Sara 01:59 Yeah. I think some of them have. And I think the historical arguments are probably the ones that have the most.

GT 02:10 As far as Church history.

Sara 02:12 Yeah, I think the role of the internet cannot be overplayed in that because the church couldn't manage in the ways that it had prior to the internet, people's access to documents and things like that. I think a lot of the history that Mike Quinn was excommunicated for is now history.

GT 02:40 Mainstream.

Sara 02:40 Yeah, that people accept. In that regard, I think there's definitely been a greater acceptance of the history. And there's also been, I think, from the Church hierarchy's perspective, it doesn't need to be about document access though that is certainly still at play. But we have our own historians who can tell these stories in ways that we think are still faith promoting. And so the Gospel Topics Essays[20] represent that.

GT 03:24 One place where there hasn't been a change, though, would you agree is scriptural historicity? We still believe in a literal Adam and Eve, Noah, Jonah. We still believe in a historical Book of Mormon. And so, anybody like Brent Metcalfe, or David Wright, that brings in historical criticism of the Bible, questions whether Noah was a real person, is that still a problem? We haven't embraced Brent Metcalfe kind of an idea or David Wright.

Sara 03:57 I haven't seen a lot of evidence of that, although there's still people, I think, talking about that. But, yeah, I haven't seen that a lot.

GT 04:06 Okay.

---

[20] See https://www.churchofjesuschrist.org/study/manual/gospel-topics-essays/essays?lang=eng

Sara 04:07 I think that there are still very firm boundaries. I think the historicity of the Scripture may be one. Women in the priesthood is certainly one. There hasn't been movement on that. There hasn't been a lot of movement on Heavenly Mother. I guess the question is how incremental we want to look at it? There's certainly more discourse about Heavenly Parents. But Renlund gave a talk[21] last year or the year before about Heavenly Mother that still very much said we don't know much about her and engaging in speculation is really dangerous, "which was a restatement of what Hinckley had been saying in the 90s.

GT 05:00 A brushback pitch maybe?

Sara 05:02 Yeah, So I think there are certain topics that the Six we're talking about that are still off limits.

GT 05:09 Okay.

Sara 05:09 Yeah.

GT 05:12 I know you also talked in your book about purity culture. That's not something that we talk about in the LDS Church. Can you talk about purity culture from your perspective and how it relates to the September Six? Do we need to quit calling it the September Six? Do we need to come up with a broader term?

Sara 05:36 No, I think we just need to be careful with the way that we remember it.

GT 05:43 It's not just six.

---

[21] See https://www.churchofjesuschrist.org/study/general-conference/2022/04/36renlund?lang=eng

Sara 05:44 It's not an anomalous thing. It was part of a much, it was a very intense moment that was part of a much broader set of events is why I'm challenging the very firm brackets that can be drawn around it. And I'm trying to say, let's not have those brackets be so firm.

Sara 06:09 The purity system that I talk about, when I was doing the research for the book, I was reading, General Conference talks and statements by Church leaders. And the word purity came up over and over again. In fact, the statement that the First Presidency and the Twelve [Apostles] issued in October 1993, addressing the September Six, said, "We are responsible for the doctrinal purity of the Church." I might not get these words exactly right. "In that we are unified." So purity, and worthiness, I think those are twin concepts, were definitely present in how the Church hierarchy was structuring, I think, the theology of the Church. Part of what I argue in the book was a purity system was put in place. That was in part a response to the rapid expansion of the Church around the globe. I think Church leaders were trying to create a center and to try to unify what they felt like was an increasingly diverse set of members. And so, I think there were a lot of activities that were trying to suggest that there was one set of beliefs. There was one way of being faithful. I include in that the Correlation process. I think that part of what you see in Correlation is the Church saying, "We're going to structure the experiences of Church members. We're going to standardize the lessons. But we're also going to structure the daily lives of believers. Make sure that being a believer isn't something you do on Sundays, but it's something that you're participating in throughout the week in the way that you live in your home and the bodily practices that you do. I think all of that was an attempt to create some unity within the Church.

GT 08:51 And so these excommunications are a way to purify the membership. Is that what is happening?

Sara 09:01 [Yes.] I think [they are] sending a message about what would and would not be acceptable.

GT 09:09 As, as an outsider, as a scholar, do you have an opinion on that? Is that a good thing? Is that a bad thing?

Sara 09:21 Do I have an opinion about it? I saw a lot of the pain that those choices caused. And so, institutions function as institutions do. But it's always important to remember that humans are part of the institutions and so humans were the ones excommunicating and humans were the ones being excommunicated. Again, institutions act as they do, but it was hard to hear some of the painful stories of people experiencing the disciplinary proceedings.

GT 10:05 I know this isn't a question you're going to want to answer, but I'm going to ask it anyway. {Rick laughing} From an outside perspective, would you have any advice on how the Church should handle intellectuals? Do you think that there should be more academic freedom or not?

Sara 10:33 Yeah, I don't know that it's my place to say, to answer that question. I do think academic freedom is important. I think it's important. I will say this, and it's something that the six were saying, so this isn't just my idea. But I think it's important. People are going to be asking questions. And so, then the question is, where can they do that? I think it's important for institutions to come up with ways that people can ask questions and feel safe in talking about them. And also, those questions can be about how the institution works. They can be about theology. I think framing questions as dangerous to faith can really limit people's ability to create fulfilling, faithful lives.

GT 11:49 You know, I look at it. Everybody loves to pull out Galileo and how he was such a heretic for thinking that the sun was the center of the universe instead of the earth. Do you see any parallels? Because I don't know anybody, any believing Catholic, Christian, Jew, anybody that they would think that the sun being the center of the universe would be faith destroying. We've come to embrace that. Is there a way? Do you see any similarities between that and some of the struggles the Church is having maybe with historicity of the Bible or the Book of Mormon? Would it be healthy for the Church to say," we don't need to fight against some of these things?"

Sara 12:44 I think that I don't have a lot to say in answer to that question. But I do think I will go back to the asking questions. I think it's important for people to be able to ask questions.

GT 12:58 Okay. Evolution, I guess would be another thing.

Sara 13:01 Yeah.

GT 13:03 So I'm trying to remember what else. What are we missing?

Sara 13:10 Well, I would say that part of how I came to understand the September Six, and this is why Mark Hofmann just does not fit. {Sara laughing}

GT 13:27 Okay.

Sara 13:31 In this larger group of dissenters that I'm talking about, I think there were people pushing back against the Church's understanding of theology, and what faithful life would look like. I see common strands in the six of arguing that God is less concerned with rules and following rules, and is more interested in creating an inclusive, egalitarian community where people can have a personal relationship with the spirit. People can be guided by their questions and can focus on figuring out the truth for themselves. Paul Toscano was one who talked about the importance of believers being able to have an active faith, rather than having the faith handed to them, being able to engage in it. And so, I just see that set of commonalities in this group. I think, really what they represent is that diversity in the Church that has been around since the very beginning.

GT 15:03 So, any last advice for people especially, say academics or people looking more in the theology? Do you have any advice for us on how to avoid any problems with our Church leaders?

Sara 15:19 Oh, gosh, I don't know. {both laughing} Again, I don't know that I should be the one giving the advice. {Sara laughing}

GT 15:25 We still like it, whether you're the one or not. I was talking to Cristina Rosetti, and we were talking about whether priests should be married and I'm like, "Well, I'll give the pope some advice here. I'm not Catholic." So, I'm giving you that opportunity as well.

Sara 15:41 Okay, so the question is?

GT 15:43 Do you have any advice for the Brent Metcalfe's and the David Wright's that may exist in the Church today? Do you just keep your head down and try not to make any waves? Do you have any advice for those kinds of people, *Gospel Tangents* listeners?

Sara 16:02 I think, in part, I see in these dissenters trying to weigh out, I think they were guided by conscience and individual relationships with the Spirit. There's a letter by Diane Wright to their stake president, where she talks about Joseph Smith as someone who was willing to seek the truth wherever it led. The Church is should be a group of people who are doing that together as a collective. I do think it's about how you frame what a faithful life looks like. I think in doing that, you are making a set of choices about your relationship to the institution.

GT 17:09 All right. Any last words?

Sara 17:11 No. Thank you for having me.

44

GT 17:13 All right. Well, why don't you show everybody the book again? Tell everybody where they can get it. *The September Six, and the Struggle for the Soul of Mormonism.* Remind us of your name.

Sara 17:22 Sara Patterson.

GT 17:23 Sara Patterson, So it's available on Amazon.[22]

Sara 17:26 [Yes,] and independent bookstores.

GT 17:28 Benchmark, I'm sure.

Sara 17:30 Yeah.

GT 17:30 Writ & Vision [Provo, UT]. Who are some of the places that you've toured recently here in Utah on your book tour.

Sara 17:37 I was just at the public library last night in Salt Lake and Writ & Vision is tomorrow.

GT 17:43 Okay, All right. Well, Dr. Sara Patterson, thank you so much for being here and *Gospel Tangents*, I really appreciate it.

Sara 17:49 Thank you.

---

[22] Can be purchased at https://amzn.to/3t1Aodc

Additional Resources:

Check out our other interviews with the September Six.

Critiquing Sept Six Book (Margaret Toscano)

Margaret Toscano discusses her experiences with the Sept 6.

945: Paul & Margaret Toscano's Reactions to Sept 6

https://gospeltangents.com/2024/06/paul-margaret-toscanos-reactions-sept-6-4-4

945: Does Excommunication Work?

https://gospeltangents.com/2024/06/does-excommunication-work-3-4/

944: Events Leading up to Sept 6

https://gospeltangents.com/2024/06/events-leading-up-sept-6-2-4/

943: Reaction to "Sept 6 & Struggle for Soul of Mormonism"

https://gospeltangents.com/2024/06/reaction-sept-6-1-4/

1st of Sept Six (Lynne Whitesides)

Lynne Whitesides was the first intellectual punished as a member of the September Six.

820: Spirituality & Family Reactions

https://gospeltangents.com/2023/09/spirituality-family-lynne-whitesides/

819: (Un)Welcome at BYU

https://gospeltangents.com/2023/09/not-the-church-i-thought-lynne-whitesides/

818: 1st of the Sept Six

https://gospeltangents.com/2023/09/first-sept-six-lynne-whitesides/

Paul Toscano's Role in Hofmann Case

Paul Toscano looks back at his roles in the Sept Six and the Hofmann Case.

https://gospeltangents.com/2023/01/paul-toscanos-role-hofmann-case/

0:00:00 Paul's Role in Hofmann Case

0:08:28 Fake plates

0:18:01 Aftermath of Christensen Death

0:23:54 Church Asked Steve to Spy on Hofmann

0:30:01 Hofmann & Fake Plates in England

0:37:18 Paul's Thoughts on Hofmann

0:45:55 Paul's Newest Novel

Paul Toscano Discusses September Six

https://gospeltangents.com/2023/01/30-years-later-sept-six/

0:00 Intro to Sept 6

6:30 Boyd K Packer's Role in Sept 6

15:13 Avraham Gileadi

18:44 Causes of Trouble

Margaret Toscano Critiques *Women and Priesthood Gospel Topics Essay*

Dr. Margaret Toscano wrote a chapter in "The Gospel Topics Series" on Women & Priesthood essay.

552: Are Church Leaders Scared of Heavenly Mother?

https://gospeltangents.com/2021/08/church-leaders-scared-mother/

551: 6 Counterpoints to Women & Priesthood Essay

https://gospeltangents.com/2021/08/6-counterpoints-women-essay/

550: Women's Spiritual vs Ecclesiastical Priesthood

https://gospeltangents.com/2021/08/spiritual-eccles-priesthood/

549: Priest or Priestesses?

Bird's Eye View of Sept Six (Janice Allred)

Janice Allred describes getting in trouble with Sept Six in 1992.

817: Advice for Church Leaders

https://gospeltangents.com/2023/09/advice-lds-church-leaders/

816: Scarlet Letter of Apostasy

https://gospeltangents.com/2023/09/scarlet-letter-apostasy/

815: From Probation to Excommunication

https://gospeltangents.com/2023/09/probation-to-excommunication/

814: Apostasy or Insubordination? Back on LDS Radar

https://gospeltangents.com/2023/09/apostasy-or-insubordination/

813: Theology of God the Mother

https://gospeltangents.com/2023/09/theology-of-god-the-mother/

Margaret Toscano on Women & Priesthood

Dr. Margaret Toscano is a Professor of Classics at University of Utah and expert on early Mormon Priesthood.

Michael Quinn – LDS Mystic & Historian

Michael Quinn discusses Wealth & Corporate Power, Sept Six, Mark Hofmann, LDS Succession, & Women & Priesthood.

Punk Rock Polygamist Talks Racism

(Moroni Jessop)

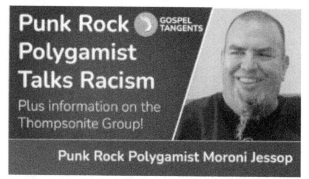

Moroni Jessop is host of "Punk Rock Polygamist" on Tik Tok & discusses his 4 excommunications and racism in Mormon fundamentalism.

812: Fundamental Racial Myths Supporting Racism

https://gospeltangents.com/2023/09/racial-myths-supporting-racism/

811: Researching Priesthood Ban Leads to DNA Tests

https://gospeltangents.com/2023/09/priesthood-ban-dna-tests/

810: Excommunicated "Lovingly" from AUB

https://gospeltangents.com/2023/09/excommunicated-over-aub-racism/

809: Encountering Independent Mormon Racism

https://gospeltangents.com/2023/09/independent-mormon-racism/

808: Growing Up & Causing LDS Trouble

https://gospeltangents.com/2023/09/growing-up-trouble-moroni-jessop/

Final Thoughts

You can get our transcripts at our amazon.com author page. I've got a link here, but just do a search for Gospel Tangents interview, and you should be able to find a bunch of them there. Please subscribe at Patreon.com/gospeltangents. For $5 a month, you can hear the entire interview uncut and for $10 you can get a pdf copy. We've also got a $15 tier where if you want a physical copy, I'll be the first to send it to you, so please subscribe at Patreon or on our website at Gospeltangents.com. For our latest updates, please like our page at facebook.com/Gospeltangents and also check our twitter updates Gospel tangents. Please subscribe on our apple podcast page tinyurl.com/GospelTangents, or you can subscribe on your android device. Just do a search for Gospel Tangents. Thanks again for listening. Click here to subscribe, here for transcript and over here we've got some more of our great videos. Thanks again.

Made in the USA
Monee, IL
22 December 2024

74924227R00036